The Yorkshire Water Way

*A journey through Yorkshire
from the Dales to the Peak District*
By Mark Reid

Volume I - Yorkshire Dales
*A 3-day walk from Kettlewell to Ilkley
via Nidderdale and the Washburn Valley.*

Scar House Reservoir

(IWP)
InnWay Publications

1

The **Yorkshire Water** Way

Volume I - Yorkshire Dales

© Mark Reid 2006
First Edition April 2006

A catalogue record for this book is available from the British Library. British Library Cataloguing in Publication Data.

All maps within this publication are based upon Ordnance Survey mapping reproduced by permission of Ordnance Survey on behalf of HMSO © Crown Copyright 2005. Ordnance Survey Licence Number: 100011978

The contents of this publication are believed correct at time of copyright. Nevertheless the author can not accept responsibility for errors and omissions, or for changes in details given. The information contained within this publication is intended only as a general guide.

Walking and outdoor activities can be strenuous and individuals must ensure that they have suitable clothing, footwear, provisions, maps and are suitably fit before starting the walk; inexperienced walkers should be supervised. You are responsible for your own safety and for others in your care, so be prepared for the unexpected - make sure you are fully equipped for the hills.

'The Inn Way' is a Registered Trademark of Mark Reid.

Published by:
INNWAY PUBLICATIONS
102 LEEDS ROAD
HARROGATE
HG2 8HB

ISBN-10:   1-902001-14-1
ISBN-13:   978-1-902001-14-2

www.innway.co.uk

A FOREWORD BY KEVIN WHITEMAN

We are fortunate in Yorkshire to have some of the country's most spectacular scenery on our doorsteps.

For many of us, heading for the hills for a long, leisurely stroll at the weekends - or perhaps to go fishing, sailing, riding or cycling - is what helps to keep us sane in a world in which so many of us spend our week days either driving a car or sitting behind a desk.

The popularity of Mark Reid's pioneering 'Inn Way' series has already underlined that walking is appealing to more and more people and, at Yorkshire Water, we are determined to delight all visitors regardless of their age, interest or ability. Indeed, the company has recently embarked on a new long-term strategy, improving key sites to further enhance our customers' enjoyment.

This book - and the second volume to follow next year - is an important step towards that goal. Most walkers want to set out, confident that they know where they are going, and who better to guide them than one of the country's best-known walking authors whose easy narrative style and simple maps have helped introduce a new generation to the Great Outdoors?

Whether readers choose to combine both books in the series and take on the entire Yorkshire Water Way in one go, tackle the walks outlined in each volume one at a time or use any of them as the basis for an afternoon's stroll, walking with Mark Reid is always a pleasure.

Of course, if you combine healthy exercise and spectacular scenery with traditional Yorkshire hospitality, there is every reason to believe both books will be well-thumbed in years to come.

We also hope people may learn a little more about the role Yorkshire Water plays in the supply of clean water to millions of people and the management of the countryside along the way.

But, if this book does nothing more than inspire people to explore the Great Outdoors and stride out for the first time, then we are a step closer to what we have set out to achieve.

Kevin Whiteman
Managing Director, Yorkshire Water

With special thanks to Steve Parsley from Yorkshire Water.

Front cover photograph: *Scar House Reservoir*
Back cover photograph: *Nidderdale from Middlesmoor churchyard.*
4-page colour insert photographs
© Mark Reid 2006

Illustrations © John A. Ives, Dringhouses, York.
www.johnaives.co.uk

Lofthouse

CONTENTS

OVERVIEW MAP

SCAR HOUSE

ANGRAM

MIDDLESMOOR

GREAT WHERNSIDE

KETTLEWELL

GOUTHWAITE

RIVER WHARFE

PATELEY BRIDGE

WHARFEDALE

NIDDERDALE

RIVER WASHBURN

RIVER NIDD

THRUSCROSS

FEWSTON

SWINSTY

WASHBURN VALLEY

LINDLEY WOOD

ILKLEY

■ OVERNIGHT STOPS

•••• ROUTE

INTRODUCTION

When you fill the kettle, turn on the shower or flush the loo, have you ever stopped to think about the long journey that water has made from its source as Pennine rainfall to fresh, clean drinking water from your tap? There is no question about it; we take our clean and waste water services for granted.

Only 200 years ago, most people drew their water from wells and threw their sewage and other household waste in open drains and rivers; taps and flush toilets were unheard of. This lack of basic hygiene meant thousands died from diseases such as cholera and dysentery and the life expectancy of even a wealthy man was lower than 50. But today, all we have to do is turn on the tap and out pours clean drinking water or flush the toilet and the waste washes away underground, out of sight. The massive infrastructure that supplies our homes and workplaces lies largely unseen underground, unless maintenance or repair disrupts our daily routine. Every day, more than 2,000 people go to work to ensure that the Yorkshire region enjoys the benefits of a modern, clean water network. In fact, Yorkshire Water is one of the ten largest water companies in the world, supplying 1.3 billion litres of drinking water through an estimated 31,000 kilometres of mains every day to an estimated 4.7 million domestic customers and 140,000 business customers. That's a lot of water! Once they have finished with it, Yorkshire Water collects and treats 136,000 tonnes of sewage daily through a network of 625 waste water treatment works.

Yorkshire Water took its current form following privatisation in 1989, inheriting its infrastructure from the public sector. Since then, the company has invested almost £1m a day on its water mains and treatment plants and developed a regional grid allowing resources to be pumped from reservoirs, rivers and groundwater sources to be used flexibly to meet demand, no matter what the weather. Leakage has also been reduced by over 440 billion litres per day - the equivalent of the daily supply to Leeds - all of which helped maintain supplies throughout the long hot summer of 2003 and the drought of 2005.

The Yorkshire Water Way is designed to combine great walking and stunning scenery with the very source of Yorkshire's water - the upland catchment areas around Yorkshire Water's 109 impounding reservoirs, which play a vital role ensuring the company has some control over the quality of water that enters its system. Yorkshire Water manages 72,000 acres of land in these reservoir catchment areas, which makes it the region's largest landowner. Since the Countryside and Rights of Way Act went onto the Statute Book in 2000, Yorkshire Water has worked ever more closely with its tenants as well as rambler groups and other recreational organisations to forge links between those given the 'right to roam' across mountain, heath and moorland and those who make a living from the land. Happily, broad swathes of the Pennines are now designated Open Access land and a new spirit of partnership is developing between the different organisations that represent recreational and commercial interests in the countryside.

The Yorkshire Water Way will take you on a journey through Yorkshire from the source of the River Nidd in the heart of the Yorkshire Dales to Langsett Reservoir in the northern Peak District, one of Yorkshire Water's most southerly reservoirs. But this walk is not just about getting from Kettlewell to Langsett; it is about the journey, not the destination. It is about the countless experiences along the way that will remain as precious memories for years to come. And perhaps whilst you are walking across the top of the Great Whernside ridge or along the banks of Fewston Reservoir, you will see for yourself where your water comes from and the role Yorkshire Water plays as a custodian of the countryside.

ROUTE DESCRIPTIONS & MAPS

ROUTE DESCRIPTIONS

The detailed route descriptions and hand-drawn maps should guide you safely along the three 'day stages' featured in this book. However, always take Ordnance Survey Explorer maps (scale 1:25,000) with you on your walks, as well as a compass or GPS. Occasionally, Rights of Way may be altered or diverted to prevent erosion damage or to improve the line of the footpath. Any changes will be clearly signposted and must be followed, and are usually marked on the most up-to-date Ordnance Survey maps.

Footpaths and bridleways are generally well maintained with good waymarking and should be marked by a signpost wherever a path leaves a public road. These signposts are often colour-coded as follows: yellow for footpaths, blue for bridleways and red for byways. Often, the path on the ground is clearly defined and easy to follow, however, some sections cross more remote areas and high moorland especially the section across Great Whernside where route-finding may be more difficult, especially in bad weather or mist.

The following abbreviations have been used throughout the route descriptions:

SP	Signpost	BW	Bridleway
FP	Footpath	FB	Footbridge

MAPS

The following Ordnance Survey Explorer maps (1:25,000) cover the three 'day stages' featured in this book.

OL30 *'Yorkshire Dales Northern & Central areas'*. This map covers Stage One from Kettlewell to Middlesmoor.

298 *'Nidderdale'*. This map covers Stage Two from Middlesmoor to Pateley Bridge, as well as part of Stage Three from Pateley Bridge to the Stone House Inn above Thruscross Reservoir.

297 *'Lower Wharfedale & Washburn Valley'*. This map covers Stage Three from Thruscross Reservoir to Ilkley.

SAFETY

Never underestimate the strenuous nature of walking particularly when this is combined with high ground and the elements. Do not attempt to complete a walk that is beyond your skill, experience or level of fitness.

Obtain a detailed weather forecast before setting out on your walk. If the weather turns bad then turn back the way you have walked. Conditions can change for the worse within minutes making walking hazardous with mist, winds and rain virtually all year round. The weather conditions on moorland can vary significantly from conditions in valleys.

Take Ordnance Survey maps (1:25,000) of the area as well as a GPS (Global Positioning System) or compass.

Your boots are the most important thing; make sure that they are waterproof, comfortable and have good ankle support and sturdy soles.

A waterproof and windproof coat and trousers are essential as well as gloves, hat and fleece for warmth. Travel light as a heavy rucksack can tire you out. Take essential items such as a fleece, snack food, first aid kit, blister plasters, sun cream, whistle, water bottle, torch and 'survival' bag. Drink plenty of fluids (not alcohol) and eat food regularly to keep energy levels up.

Always walk in a group unless you are very experienced and inform someone of your route and report your safe arrival. In an emergency summon help with six blasts of your whistle or call the police (who will contact the mountain rescue team) giving details of the incident and location.

Take care when crossing rivers or roads and walk in single file (facing oncoming traffic) when walking along country lanes. Do not explore old mine or quarry workings.

When walking through grassy moorland keep a watchful eye for adders, Britain's only poisonous snake. If bitten, seek medical help immediately.

Above all, keep your hands out of your pockets and look where you are going! REMEMBER: "An experienced walker knows when to turn back"

COUNTRYSIDE CODE

Consider other people
Showing consideration and respect for other people makes the countryside a pleasant environment for everyone – at home, at work and at leisure.

Enjoy the countryside and respect its life and work
We have a responsibility to protect our countryside now and for future generations. Tread gently – discover the beauty of the natural environment and take care not to damage, destroy or remove features such as rocks, plants and trees. Do not touch crops, machinery or livestock.

Leave gates and property as you find them
Please respect the working life of the countryside, as our actions can affect people's livelihoods, our heritage, and the safety and welfare of animals and ourselves. Use stiles and gates to cross fences and walls and close gates behind you.

Keep to public Rights of Way or Open Access areas
Footpaths are for walkers; bridleways are for cyclists, horse-riders and walkers. Motorbikes and cars should keep to roads.

Do not make excessive noise
The hills and valleys should be quiet places.

Safeguard water supplies
Streams are used by livestock and often feed reservoirs for drinking supplies.

Guard against risk of fire
Uncontrolled fires can devastate grassy hillsides or moorland.

Keep dogs under control
A loose dog can be catastrophic for ground-nesting birds, sheep and sometimes the dog itself. By law, farmers are entitled to destroy a dog that injures or worries their animals.

Take litter home
Litter is dangerous and unsightly.

Safety
Weather can change quickly; are you fully equipped for the hills?

USEFUL INFORMATION

If you are travelling by public transport make sure that you check train and bus times before you set out as these often vary seasonally. Book accommodation in advance as B&B's can get fully booked up during the summer months and may close temporarily during the winter months.

InnWay Publications Website: *www.innway.co.uk*
A comprehensive site with detailed information to help organise your walk.

Yorkshire Tourist Board Website: *www.yorkshirevisitor.com*
A comprehensive site for tourists visiting Yorkshire, including accommodation.

Yorkshire Water   0845 1 24 24 24
PO Box 52
Bradford
BD3 7YD
Website: www.yorkshirewater.com

Yorkshire Dales National Park Information Centre:
Grassington Information Centre: 01756 751690

Tourist Information Centres: (T.I.C.)
Harrogate   01423 537300
Ilkley   01943 602319
Pateley Bridge   01423 711147
Skipton   01756 792809

Public Transport:
Public Transport Traveline: 0870 608 2 608
A 'one stop' information line for national, regional and local bus and train services.
Website: www.traveline.org.uk

Rail Enquiries   08457 484950
There are railway stations at Harrogate, Ilkley and Skipton.
Website: www.nationalrail.co.uk

ACCOMMODATION & FACILITIES
AT THE OVERNIGHT STOPS

KETTLEWELL

How to get to Kettlewell:
Public Transport: The nearest train station is at Skipton, from where there are frequent bus services to Kettlewell via Grassington. *For public transport information call Traveline on 0870 608 2 608 or www.traveline.org.uk*

Kettlewell is a thriving Dales village with a good selection of pubs, B&B's and shops including an outdoor shop, Post Office, general stores, gift shops, café and garage. There is also a Youth Hostel and campsite in the village, as well as a National Park Information Point, toilets, payphone and large car park.

For accommodation contact:
National Park Information Centre at Grassington: 01756 751690

MIDDLESMOOR

Middlesmoor is a delightful Dales village perched high on a shoulder of land overlooking Upper Nidderdale. The village boasts a small car park, public payphone, toilets, campsite (behind the Crown Hotel) and the Crown Hotel, which has seven letting bedrooms. There is a large campsite at Studfold Farm near How Stean Gorge as well as accommodation available at the Crown Hotel at Lofthouse, both of which are on the route of the following day's walk.

For accommodation contact:
Tourist Information Centre at Pateley Bridge (01423 711147)
or Harrogate (01423 537300)

PATELEY BRIDGE

Pateley Bridge is a thriving small Dales town with an abundance of facilities and amenities including several B&B's, hotels, pubs, Tourist Information Centre, Post Office, chemist, newsagent, HSBC and Barclays banks, restaurants, garage, fish & chip shop, cafés, delicatessen, general stores, craft and gift shops, The Playhouse theatre, Nidderdale Museum, toilets, car parks, recreation ground and campsite.

For accommodation contact:
Tourist Information Centre at Pateley Bridge (01423 711147)
or Harrogate (01423 537300)

Blubberhouses

If you wish, you can to divide the Stage Three walk from Pateley Bridge to Ilkley over two days by staying overnight at Blubberhouses where you will find a B&B (Scaife Hall Farm: 01943 880354) as well as the Hopper Lane Hotel (01943 880246). This pub is located half a mile to the east of Blubberhouses along the A59 towards Harrogate.

ILKLEY

The former spa town of Ilkley is elegant and refined with wide streets, pleasant gardens and interesting shops. Ilkley boasts an abundance of facilities including hotels, B&B's, pubs, restaurants, cafés, delicatessens, general stores, supermarkets, craft and gift shops, several banks, outdoor shop, the Manor House Museum, Tourist Information Centre and a train station with regular services to Leeds.

For accommodation contact:
Tourist Information Centre at Ilkley: 01943 602319

How to get from Ilkley:
Public Transport: There is a train station at Ilkley with regular trains to Leeds. *For public transport information call National Rail Enquiries on 08457 484950 or Traveline on 0870 608 2 608 www.traveline.org.uk*

*All of the above information is for guide purposes only and many facilities are liable to change. **If it is important – check it.***

- Kettlewell to Middlesmoor -

WALK INFORMATION

Highlights
: Ketel's spring, England's highest chapel, the place to get a millstone, the source of the Nidd, a high ridge between two dales, wonderful views and wild landscapes, a most terrible murder, Bradford's water supply, towering stone walls, a forgotten village, old packhorse routes, an ancient preaching cross and the finest view of Nidderdale.

Distance
: Kettlewell to Middlesmoor   11 miles

Time
: 5 - 6 hours

Grid References
: Grid References have been given to assist route finding; for example the Grid Reference for Kettlewell Church is SD 972 723.

Refreshments
: Pubs at Kettlewell and Middlesmoor. Shops at Kettlewell. No facilities en route - take plenty of provisions and water with you.

Terrain
: Clear grassy paths lead steadily up from Kettlewell above Dowber Gill (steep drops to the side of the path in places) to reach Hag Dyke Farm, from where a boggy path climbs steeply up across open moorland onto the summit ridge of Great Whernside. The summit is exposed to the elements. A boggy / rocky path follows the summit ridge for almost 2 miles before a fairly steep descent into a 'saddle' of land in the shadow of Little Whernside from where a bridleway turns off across rough boggy moorland

skirting across the flanks of Little Whernside to reach a stony track just above Scar House Reservoir. This track is followed down over the dam wall, after which a rough stony track heads steeply up across the outcrops of Woodale Scar, then across the exposed moorland of In Moor to reach Middlesmoor.

Ascents   Great Whernside - 704 metres above sea level
In Moor - 434 metres above sea level

Caution   This is a strenuous walk up to the summit of Great Whernside with some steep sections across rough, rocky ground. The walk along the top of the ridge of Great Whernside is exposed to the elements, with rough boggy ground underfoot. Navigation may be difficult in poor weather - OS Map and compass / GPS essential. The bridleway across the flanks of Little Whernside is boggy underfoot with hidden hollows and streams. The track from Scar House Reservoir onto In Moor is steep and rocky in places.

PUBS ALONG THE WALK

Kings Head, Kettlewell: 01756 760242
Blue Bell Hotel, Kettlewell: 01756 760230
Racehorses Hotel, Kettlewell: 01756 760233
Crown Hotel, Middlesmoor: 01423 755204

FACILITIES ALONG THE WALK

Kettlewell   Inn / B&B / Shop / P.O. / Café / Bus / Phone / Toilets / Camp / Youth Hostel
Scar House Reservoir   Toilets
Middlesmoor   Inn / Bus / Phone / Toilets / Camp

ROUTE DESCRIPTION

(Map One)

From the car park behind the garage near the bridge across the River Wharfe at Kettlewell (SD 968 723), turn left along the main road into the centre of Kettlewell bearing left over the bridge across Cam Gill Beck immediately after which turn right (Blue Bell Inn in front of you) and follow the lane up through the village to reach a junction with the General Stores on the corner. Turn right here, over another bridge then immediately left along a lane (King's Head on your right). Follow this lane alongside Cam Gill Beck up to reach a small stone bridge to your left on the edge of the village. Do not cross this bridge, but continue straight on along the rough track (SP 'Hag Dyke, Providence Pot'), still with the stream on your left, to reach another stone bridge across Dowber Gill Beck. Cross this bridge then turn immediately right (SP 'Hag Dyke') along a streamside path to quickly reach a wall-stile and gate to your left. Cross the stile then head straight on (SP 'Hag Dyke') along a wide grassy path climbing up alongside the wall on your left to reach a wall-stile at the top of the field. After this stile, carry straight on along the grassy path up through a gate in a wall, after which follow the path climbing quite steeply up to reach a ladder stile beside a large wall-gap. Cross the stile then head straight on along the wide path bearing very slightly to the right up to reach an 'edge' of land high above Dowber Gill Beck (SP), with steep drops to the side of the path into this narrow valley. The path now levels out and leads on through two bridlegates and over a ladder stile before climbing up again (SP) then bending to the right through a large gap in a wall up to reach Hag Dyke (SD 990 733).

Turn right through the gate into the yard of Hag Dyke (SP 'Coverdale Road via Great Whernside') then follow the path immediately to the right of the old farm buildings through a small gate, then head left through another gate passing behind the old farmhouse along a distinct path climbing quickly but steeply up a rocky escarpment onto a flat plateau (surmounted by a line of stone cairns). Head straight on along the clearly waymarked path (marker posts) as it meanders across the gently rising boggy moorland - *boulder-strewn summit ridge of Great Whernside directly ahead.* As you reach the foot of the steep summit ridge, follow the path slanting quite steeply up to the right across the steep bank then, where the gradient eases slightly, head straight up across the boulder-strewn hillside to reach the rocky escarpment and the summit plateau of Great Whernside with its large cairn and trig point (SE 002 739)

At the trig point on the summit turn left and follow the path across the flat plateau of Great Whernside keeping close to the rocky escarpment on your left. The path soon divides with a waymarked path slanting off to the left - our route continues straight on along the top of the rocky escarpment passing a large stone cairn, then a stone shelter and on to reach the conspicuous outcrop of Blackfell Crags. Continue straight on dropping gradually down across the top of the wide 'shoulder' of land to reach the corner of a wall at Nidd Head (SD 998 752). Carry straight on alongside this wall on your left (ignore the stile by the wall corner) to soon reach a wall across your path. Head through the small gap in this wall then carry straight on along the top of the ridge alongside the wall on your left for a further 0.5 miles to reach another tumbledown wall across your path, after which the path begins to drop down gently at first then quite steeply (still with the wall on your left) into the 'saddle' of land between the Great Whernside ridge and Little Whernside (fine views across Coverdale ahead). As you near the bottom of the steep bank you pass a bridlegate in the wall to your left, marked by a waymarker post (SE 009 764), where you carry straight on along the wide rough path bearing very slightly away from the wall gradually dropping down (with the wall now across to your left) into the bottom of the 'saddle' of land. As you reach the lowest point of the 'saddle' you pass a very small 'dog leg' in the wall across to your left, at which point branch off to the right along the wide rough path (away from the wall and ridge) heading across the rough grassy moorland down towards Nidderdale.

(Map Two)
Follow this wide, rough path heading across boggy moorland (waymarker post), with the broad valley of the infant River Nidd

sweeping away down to your right, meandering across the rough hillside to reach a tumbledown wall across your path after 0.75 miles (waymarker post - SE 024 769). Cross the wall and continue along the boggy path (hidden hollows and streams) skirting across the foot of the steep hillside of Hard Bank on your left (upper flanks of Little Whernside), with gently shelving moorland sweeping away to your right, to reach a gate in a wall across your path (Scar House Reservoir comes into view). Head through the gate and follow the clear boggy path straight on meandering across the gently shelving grassy moorland (dam wall of Angram Reservoir comes into view to your right) then gradually drop down across the hillside (heading towards the copse of trees to the left of the reservoir) to reach a tumbledown wall across your path just after a ford across Wench Gill (SE 039 773). Head through the wall and follow the path straight on bearing slightly to the right down to reach a small gap in the wall to your right, after which head left and follow the path keeping close to the wall on your left down to reach a walled track beside a bridge across Trows Beck and a junction of tracks. Turn left over the bridge, immediately after which turn right along the walled track to reach the ruins of Lodge set amongst the copse of trees (SE 049 773).

(Map Three)
Continue straight on along the enclosed stony track leaving the ruins of Lodge behind and follow this straight on skirting across the lower flanks of Dead Man's Hill for 1 mile, with Scar House Reservoir down to your right, down to join a metalled road beside the dam wall of this reservoir. Cross the dam wall then turn right (SP 'Nidderdale Way') and follow the lane straight on with the reservoir now to your right for about 300 yards then, just before the gate across the lane, turn left back on yourself along a rough stony track (SP 'Middlesmoor' - SE 065 766). Follow this stony track climbing up across the valley side then winding steeply up across the outcrops of Woodale Scar onto the moorland of Scar House Pasture. Follow the unenclosed track across the moorland to soon reach a gate across the track at the start of the walled track of In Moor Lane. Follow this clear walled track straight on, gently dropping down across In Moor for 1.75 miles to reach Middlesmoor (SE 093 743).

MAP ONE

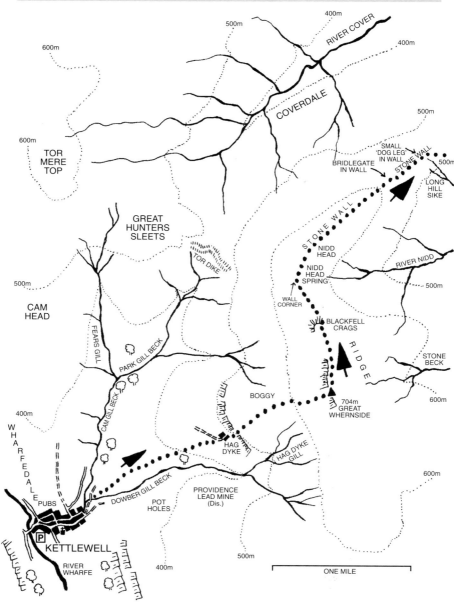

MAP TWO

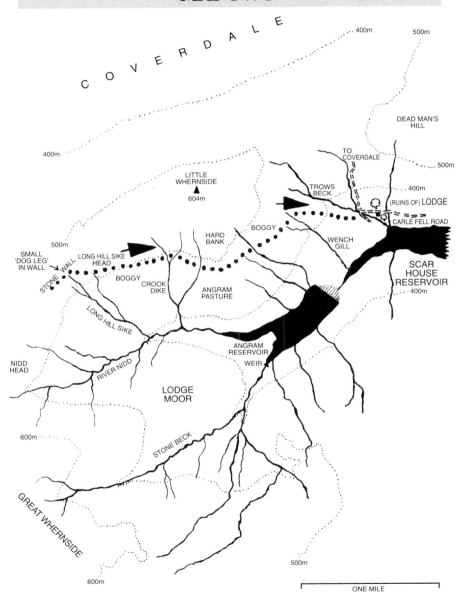

21

MAP THREE

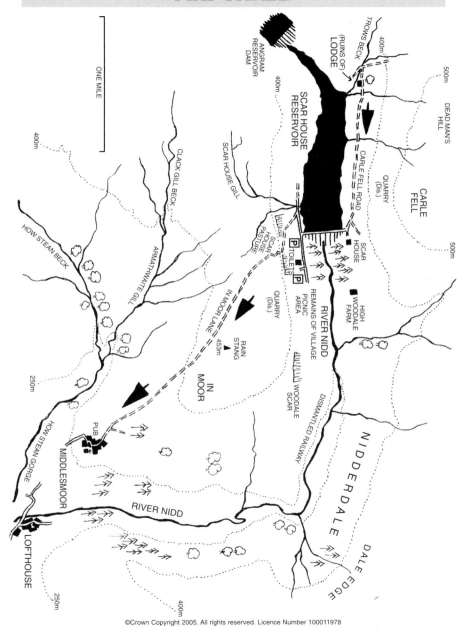

TROWS BECK

(RUINS OF) LODGE

400m

500m

DEAD MAN'S HILL

ANGRAM RESERVOIR DAM

400m

SCAR HOUSE RESERVOIR

ONE MILE

400m

SCAR HOUSE GILL

CLACK GILL BECK

CARLE FELL ROAD

QUARRY (Dis.)

CARLE FELL

500m

ARMATHWAITE GILL

HOW STEAN BECK

SCAR HOUSE PASTURE

P TOILETS

P

SCAR HOUSE

RIVER NIDD

HIGH WOODALE FARM

IN MOOR LANE

QUARRY (Dis.)

PICNIC AREA

REMAINS OF VILLAGE

250m

RAIN STANG

453m

IN MOOR

WOODALE SCAR

DISMANTLED RAILWAY

PUB

N I D D E R D A L E

HOW STEAN GORGE

MIDDLESMOOR

RIVER NIDD

D A L E   E D G E

LOFTHOUSE

250m

400m

22

POINTS OF INTEREST

KETTLEWELL

Kettlewell is one of the finest villages in the Yorkshire Dales, a delightful cluster of old cottages and inns sheltered in the side-valley of Cam Gill Beck near its confluence with the River Wharfe. A maze of lanes and paths entice you to explore the heart of the village which straddles Cam Gill Beck some distance up into the deep cleft of its valley, with numerous old bridges spanning the fast-flowing tumbling waters. First settled by a Norse-Irish chieftain called 'Ketel' back in the 9th Century, the village grew in importance following the granting of lands in the area to the monks of Coverham Abbey in the 12th Century. Fountains Abbey and Bolton Priory also owned land nearby which, combined with its strategic location at the junction of several important routes, meant that Kettlewell quickly grew into an important trading centre and was granted a market charter in the 13th Century. These routes included the old Roman road from Ilkley to Bainbridge, the monastic route over to Coverham Abbey via Top Mere Road, numerous packhorse trails and, later, the stagecoach route from London, all of which brought a steady stream of travellers, drovers and tradesmen into the village.

During the 18th and 19th centuries, lead mining flourished in the hills above Kettlewell and brought prosperity to the village with many houses either rebuilt or improved during the height of this industrial activity, although only a handful of older 17th Century cottages remain. Soon, a bustling village grew with as many as thirteen inns to accommodate the market-goers, miners and travellers. The market lapsed long ago; however, three inns remain including the King's Head with its wonderful inglenook fireplace, the Blue Bell Hotel which dates back to 1680 and was originally a coaching inn that takes its name from one of the old stagecoach companies. Across the road from the Blue Bell Hotel stands the Racehorses Hotel, which was once used as the stables for the stagecoaches as the 'trace horses' were used to pull the coaches up the steep Park Rash Pass behind the village.

The Church of St Mary dates back to Norman times; however, it was 'restored' in Victorian times so much that only fragments of this earlier church survive including the original Norman font. Inside, there is a framed document from 1380 concerning the monks of Coverham Abbey whilst in the churchyard is the grave of a local man who died in 1770 at the age of 117! Today, Kettlewell is a thriving village that retains its own identity despite the large number of visitors. Not only is it one of the finest bases in the Yorkshire Dales for walking with paths radiating in every direction, but it also hosts a scarecrow festival every August and was recently used as a location in the film 'Calendar Girls'.

HAG DYKE

On the climb up to the summit of Great Whernside you come rather unexpectedly across the 18th Century farmhouse of Hag Dyke, used as a Scout Hostel since 1947. This is the highest building in the former West Riding of Yorkshire and one of the highest in the country. It even has its own chapel in a converted hay-barn that stands as the highest chapel in England, opened in 1954 to serve the scout groups that use Hag Dyke. The old farmhouse is reputedly haunted!

GREAT WHERNSIDE

Great Whernside towers above Upper Wharfedale, an immense mountainous shoulder of high moorland that separates Wharfedale from Nidderdale; this is Wharfedale's highest fell and one of the finest in the Yorkshire Dales. The boulder-strewn flat summit ridge is a rocky shelf of gritstone, punctuated by boulders and crags including Blackfell Crags - many of the broad rises along the ridge look higher than the actual 'summit' which is identifiable by its large cairn and OS Trig Point. This cap of gritstone across the high summit ridge sits on top of the underlying limestone strata that dominates the landscape of Upper Wharfedale - it is this gritstone that gave the mountain its name for Whernside means 'the hillside where millstones were got'. Great Whernside is often mistaken for Whernside above Ribblehead, which forms one of the famous Three Peaks of Yorkshire: Whernside (736 metres), Ingleborough (724 metres) and Pen-y-ghent (694 metres). Great Whernside is 10 metres higher than Pen-y-ghent with the added benefit of far fewer walkers aiming for its summit and some of the best fell-walking in the Yorkshire Dales.

From Kettlewell, a wonderful grassy path heads steadily up alongside the deep cleft of Dowber Gill Beck as far as Hag Dyke, from where a boggy moorland path gradually climbs up towards the line of crags across the summit before a final steep pull up onto the summit ridge. From this high vantage point some 704 metres above sea level incredible views unfold in every direction with fells, hills and mountains rising and falling as far as the eye can see with superb views across Wharfedale towards Kilnsey Crag, down along the length of Coverdale towards Leyburn and across towards Buckden Pike (702 metres). On a clear day, a wonderful panorama of famous fells unfolds with (from south to north) Simon's Seat, Pendle Hill, Fountains Fell, Pen-y-ghent, Ingleborough, Whernside, Buckden Pike and the Lakeland mountains on the horizon.

NIDD HEAD
From the summit of Great Whernside, a fine ridge walk ensues northwards gradually dropping down across the gently shelving ridge passing Blackfell Crags to join a corner of a stone wall at Nidd Head; this wall forms the eastern boundary of the Yorkshire Dales National Park. From here, a wonderful view unfolds to the east of the twin reservoirs of Upper Nidderdale cradled amongst rolling fells. About 400 yards to the east of this wall corner is Nidd Head Spring where the River Nidd is born amongst boggy peat hags and rough grassy moorland. The Nidd has the rare distinction of being named a river from its source and is derived from an ancient Celtic word meaning 'brilliant' or 'shining'. Open Access land means that you can now seek out this spring and dip your boot into it for good measure! Our route continues alongside this wall for another mile or so down into the saddle of moorland between the Great Whernside ridge and Little Whernside to reach an old packhorse route across this saddle of land between Coverdale and Nidderdale - a superb view down the length of Coverdale unfolds as you drop down into this saddle. This old trail, now a bridleway, leads steadily down across the flanks of Little Whernside through an untamed landscape of wild moorland and hidden gills to eventually reach the ruinous buildings at Lodge just above Scar House Reservoir. It is a

wonderful walk across wild fells with the broad valley of the infant River Nidd sweeping away towards the huge bulk of Great Whernside.

When the boundaries of the Yorkshire Dales National Park were being drawn up in the early 1950s, Nidderdale was inexplicably excluded. The reason given was that the three large reservoirs that flood stretches of the upper valley were not natural features. Strange logic indeed, as Nidderdale is a valley of neat stone villages, wild gritstone moors, limestone gorges and deep valleys; the grand reservoirs only add to the attraction giving this valley wonderful views and landscapes not found in any of the other main river valleys of the Yorkshire Dales. Much of Nidderdale is now protected as an Area of Outstanding Natural Beauty, and its lack of national park status means that it is often much quieter and peaceful than neighbouring Wharfedale.

LODGE
The remains of the hamlet of Lodge can be found amongst a copse of trees beside the stony track of Carle Fell Road. This is actually an old County Road that leads across the moors over to Horsehouse in Coverdale, once busy with drovers, traders, packhorses and travellers. In medieval times a hunting lodge stood on this site, later rebuilt as a wayside inn that offered food, refreshment and accommodation for these travellers. According to the Yorkshire historian Ella Pontefract ('Wensleydale' 1936), during the 18th Century, a group of travelling tradesmen from Scotland came over the moors from Coverdale and called into the inn for refreshment - they were not seen again until their headless bodies were found buried in the peat on the moors above the inn, since when the particular stretch of moorland has been known as Dead Man's Hill.

ANGRAM & SCAR HOUSE RESERVOIRS
Cradled by the high fells of Upper Nidderdale in the shadow of the mighty bulk of Great Whernside, the man-made reservoirs of Angram and Scar House stand out starkly against the wild and untamed landscape. The dams are impressive with two huge gritstone walls rising over 200-ft above the deep V-shaped valley trapping the waters of the infant River Nidd. These reservoirs are set amongst one of Yorkshire

Water's largest landholdings, with mile upon mile of uninhabited moorland rising up towards the Great Whernside ridge that provides the perfect catchment area for clean, fresh Yorkshire water. The main feeder streams are Stone Beck and the River Nidd which, along with countless other tumbling becks, flow down into these reservoirs; Angram has a capacity of over 1,000 million gallons whilst Scar House traps 2,200 million gallons of water. The dam wall of Scar House Reservoir stretches for a third of a mile across the valley and contains over one million tonnes of masonry - the stone was quarried on Carle Fell to the north side of the valley above the dam wall. Water is carried from these two supply reservoirs by gravity via the 31-mile Nidd Aqueduct all the way to the water treatment works at Chellow Heights near Bradford, from where it is distributed to homes throughout this great West Riding city.

The first reservoir to be built in Nidderdale was Gouthwaite above Pateley Bridge, completed in 1901 as a compensation reservoir for these two supply reservoirs at the head of the valley. Angram Reservoir was completed in 1919 whilst Scar House Reservoir was finished in 1936. A large village was built beside Scar House dam to house the workers with shops, cinema, concert hall, gymnasium, church, small hospital and housing for 1,250 people; the foundations of Scar Village can still be seen around the present car park and toilets. Materials were brought to this remote site via the Nidd Valley Light Railway that operated from the North Eastern Railway terminus at Pateley Bridge. Built in 1907 by Bradford Corporation, the NVLR also carried a passenger service as far as Lofthouse; this was the only passenger-carrying service operated by a municipality in the country. The line closed in 1936 when Scar House was completed, although its route can still be traced.

For short circular walks around these reservoirs:
Scar House & Angram walk (low-level route: 4 miles / high-level route: 8.5 miles)
www.yorkshirewater.com/?OBH=522&ID=2059

IN MOOR LANE

From Scar House Reservoir, an old track leads steeply up across the outcrops of Woodale Scar onto the open moorland of Scar House Pasture, with huge gritstone boulders precariously balanced above your head! Superb views unfold with every step back across the reservoir framed by the bulk of Little Whernside. Many years ago, this track was a busy packhorse route over the fells to Coverdale via Lodge, although the section of the route where it crossed the River Nidd is now submerged beneath the waters of the reservoir. After this initial climb, the track heads across the open moorland of Scar House Pasture before it becomes a walled track that leads steadily down to Middlesmoor, a wonderful track across breezy heights with glorious views down the length of Nidderdale and Gouthwaite Reservoir sparkling in the distance. To the west, a vast landscape of open moorland stretches for mile upon mile towards Great Whernside and the conspicuous rise of Meugher (575 metres) at the head of the valley of How Stean Beck. You can not help but glance back at this mighty ridge of moorland and feel rather pleased that you have just walked over it from Kettlewell!

MIDDLESMOOR

The windswept village of Middlesmoor has a commanding position high above the valley, situated on a great promontory of moorland known as In Moor between Nidderdale and the valley of How Stean Beck. It can only be reached by a steep, twisting road, which makes this one of the most exposed and windswept villages in the Yorkshire Dales some 300-metres (1,000-ft) above sea level. The road ends here, for only a rough track continues across the moors over to the reservoirs of Upper Nidderdale. The village is a delightful jumble of old cottages and alleyways, which makes it an interesting place to explore with St Chad's Church hidden away along a cobbled lane. The houses and farms of Middlesmoor are built in the local vernacular style using dark gristone and have a wonderful simplicity as well as common style that give the village a real sense of unity; the village feels as though it is part of the landscape. It is a special place where the rest of the world seems far away, in both time and space, and the Crown Hotel is the perfect place to soak up this unique atmosphere, a classic Dales inn with flagstone floor, roaring fires, cosy corners and good local ale.

The view from the churchyard is superb with the whole of Nidderdale laid out before you and Gouthwaite Reservoir shimmering in the distance, one of the finest views in the Yorkshire Dales. This site has been a place of worship since Saxon times, perhaps earlier as the circular churchyard suggests Pagan origins. It was not until medieval times that the village of Middlesmoor began to develop around a grange, or monastic farm, which belonged to Byland Abbey, although most of the buildings we see today date from the 18th and 19th centuries when farming and lead mining were the mainstays of the local economy. Despite this monastic connection, the village did not have its own chapel until 1484 before which villagers had to make the long and difficult journey across the moors to the nearest parish church at Kirkby Malzeard some ten miles away for their hatches, matches and dispatches! This 15th Century church was later extensively restored in 1866 to create the present church. Inside, there is an Anglo-Saxon font as well as a finely carved Saxon cross thought to have been erected in the churchyard by St Chad himself as a preaching cross to convert the local pagans. St Chad was a disciple of Aidan, one of the famed Lindisfarne monks, and he later became Abbot of Lastingham in Yorkshire and finally Bishop of Mercia (Lichfield) during the 7th Century.

Middlesmoor Church

STAGE TWO
- Middlesmoor to Pateley Bridge -

WALK INFORMATION

Highlights

England's Little Switzerland, a dry river, cures to keep the doctor away, fine views from a grand shooting lodge, old roads and wild moorland, Jenny Twigg and her daughter Tib, migratory birds on the mudflats of Gouthwaite, the only municipal railway in the country and along the banks of the Nidd.

Distance

Middlesmoor to Bouthwaite	7 miles
Bouthwaite to Pateley Bridge	4.5 miles
Total	11.5 miles

Time

5 - 6 hours

Grid References

Grid References have been given to assist route finding; for example the Grid Reference for Middlesmoor Church is SE 093 742.

Refreshments

Pubs at Middlesmoor, Lofthouse, Ramsgill, Wath and Pateley Bridge. Cafés at How Stean Gorge and Pateley Bridge. Shops at Lofthouse and Pateley Bridge.

Terrain

From Middlesmoor, field paths and quiet country lanes lead to Lofthouse, from where a grassy / muddy track leads to Thrope Farm. There is then a steep climb along a grassy bridleway onto the moorland of Thrope Edge (superb views) from where clear stony tracks lead across Fountains Earth Moor for several miles gradually dropping down to reach Bouthwaite at the top of Gouthwaite Reservoir. The final descent into Bouthwaite is quite steep along a clear but rough track. From Bouthwaite, a metalled farm lane then a muddy track skirts the shores of Gouthwaite Reservoir passing the dam wall from where a clear riverside path leads all the way to Pateley Bridge.

Ascents   Thrope Edge - 400 metres above sea level

Caution   The climb up onto Thrope Edge is steep, although the path is clear. This walk follows clear tracks across Fountains Earth Moor which are exposed to the elements, although route finding is relatively easy.

PUBS ALONG THE WALK

Crown Hotel, Middlesmoor:	01423 755204
Crown Hotel, Lofthouse:	01423 755206
Yorke Arms, Ramsgill:	01423 755243
Sportsman's Arms, Wath:	01423 711306
Crown Inn, Pateley Bridge:	01423 712455
Royal Oak, Pateley Bridge:	01423 711577
Harefield Hall Hotel, Pateley Bridge:	01423 711429

FACILITIES ALONG THE WALK

Middlesmoor	Inn / Bus/ Phone / Toilets / Camp
How Stean Gorge	Café / Phone/ Camp
Lofthouse	Inn / Shop / P.O. / Bus / Phone / Toilets
Ramsgill	Inn / Bus / Phone
Wath	Inn / Bus / Phone
Pateley Bridge	Inn / B&B / Shop / P.O. / Café / Bus / Phone / Toilets / Camp

ROUTE DESCRIPTION

(Map Four)

From the Crown Hotel at Middlesmoor (SE 093 743), follow the road down through the village passing the red 'phone box and carry on along the road winding steeply down out of Middlesmoor. As the road levels out at the bottom of the steep hill below the village, take the footpath to the right through a squeeze-stile beside a gate (signpost 'Stean'). Head straight down across two fields (through two squeeze-stiles) alongside the field boundary on your right; at the third field, carry straight on for a short distance then turn right through a squeeze-stile in the wall on your right. After this squeeze-stile, bear left down across the field to reach a small gate above the wooded ravine of How Stean Beck. Drop down over a footbridge across the stream then follow the clear path straight on up to reach a squeeze-stile that leads out onto a small field (caravan in the field). Bear right across this small field to reach a squeeze-stile in the corner that leads onto the road (hamlet of Stean just across to your right - SE 089 735).

Turn left along the road and follow this down, passing the entrance to How Stean Gorge on your left, then carry on down along the road (with How Stean Beck on your left) to reach a road-bridge to your left across How Stean Beck (with the entrance to Studfold Farm ahead). Turn left across this bridge and follow the road winding up to reach a T-junction with the main valley road (SE 098 735). Turn right along the road towards 'Lofthouse' then, where the road curves round to the right after a short distance, head straight on (on this bend) through the right-hand of two gates. Bear right across the field then skirt to the left around an old stone barn (cricket pitch on your right) to reach a gate that leads onto a road (Yorkshire Water road to Scar House and Angram reservoirs). Cross over the road and head straight on along the track opposite (to the left of the garages), through a squeeze-stile beside a gate and over a bridge across the River Nidd, after which follow the path up to the right to emerge in the centre of Lofthouse beside the Memorial Water Fountain (SE 101 735).

Turn left along the road (passing the Post Office) up out of the village and continue up along the unfenced road leaving Lofthouse behind then, where the road bends up to the right after 250 yards, head straight on (to the left) along the grassy track (signpost 'Scar House Res.') that leads to a gate in a wall (SE 102 738). Head through the gate and follow the grassy track straight on then, where the track forks after a short distance, follow the left-hand track straight on. Follow this clear track (Thrope Lane) through woodland then across the open hillside with the River Nidd down to your left (superb views across Upper Nidderdale) for 0.75 miles to reach Thrope Farm (track becomes enclosed by walls as you approach the farm). Just as you reach the farmhouse turn right through a series of three gates heading up through some livestock pens and out onto a field beside a stone barn, then head straight up the field keeping fairly close to the wall on your right to reach a gate in a fence at the top of the field. After the gate, turn sharp left alongside the fence for about 25 yards then, as you reach a small section of wall on your left in this fence, turn right heading steeply up the hillside alongside a line of old fence posts. Follow the bridleway climbing steeply up through sparse birchwood, with a small dry 'valley' and plantation to your right, then follow the path as it bends sharply round to the left and slants steadily up across the steep hillside to reach a gate in a wall below the outcrops of Thrope Edge, with the ornate shooting house with its castellated tower on the ridge ahead (SE 106 753). Head through the gate and follow the rough path bearing to the left up the hillside (heading towards the left side of the shooting house) then gently curving round to the right heading up onto the top of Thrope Edge just to the left of the shooting house. As you reach the top of Thrope Edge (with the shooting house just to your right) carry straight on up across the moorland to quickly join a stony shooters' track. Turn right along this track passing behind the shooting house along the top of Thrope Edge then bending to the left away from the Edge (joins a wall on your right) and follow this track straight on for 0.5 miles to join the moorland road of Pott Moor High Road (SE 114 749).

Turn left along the road for 75 yards then take the walled track to the right. Follow this track straight on up to reach a gate across the track after just over 0.25 miles, after which carry straight on along the track (with the wall now just on your right and open moorland on your left) then, where this wall bends to the right and the track forks, follow the right-hand grassy track heading downhill alongside the wall on the right. Follow this track straight on heading steadily down across Fountains Earth Moor for just over 0.5 miles to reach a gate across the track (SE 124 739). Head through the gate and carry straight on along the track (now enclosed by walls on either side) heading gradually down for a further mile, with Sypeland Crags across to your left, over a bridge across Sypeland Gill then on to reach a large stone-built bridge across Lul Beck, after which follow the track round to the right up to reach a gate at the end of the enclosed track (walls on either side end - SE 136 727). Just after this gate you reach a 'junction' with another track - follow the track to the right (alongside the wall on your right) passing above a plantation then on for a further 0.5 miles to reach a T-junction with another track. Turn right ('Unsuitable for Motors' sign) and follow the clear rough track heading steadily down the hillside for 1 mile (Gouthwaite Reservoir comes into view after a while) to reach a crossroads of lanes and tracks in the hamlet of Bouthwaite (SE 124 712). *10-minute detour to the Yorke Arms at Ramsgill – at this crossroads head straight on along the lane down to reach the main valley road where you head left over Nidd Bridge into Ramsgill. Re-trace your steps back to this crossroads in Bouthwaite.*

(Map Five)
At the crossroads of tracks and lanes at Bouthwaite, turn left along the metalled lane (signpost 'Wath') and follow this out of the hamlet heading towards Gouthwaite Reservoir. Follow this lane for 0.75 miles skirting the banks of Gouthwaite Reservoir to reach the cluster of farms, cottages and buildings of Covill Grange Farm and Covill House Farm (SE 129 703). As you enter the hamlet, continue straight on along the lane over the bridge across Byerbeck Gill (made from railway sleepers) then, where the metalled lane ends just beyond the houses, carry straight on along the enclosed track ahead. Follow this track straight on (enclosed by stone walls) down to join the banks of the reservoir and on to reach a gate at the end of the walled track (stone walls on either side

end). Head through the gate and carry straight on along the track for about 100 yards then, where the track forks, follow the right-hand track straight on (enclosed by fencing) along the banks of the reservoir. Carry on along the track for about 0.5 miles then, where the fencing ends, follow the track gradually rising up across the hillside (joins a stone wall on your right) with Gouthwaite Reservoir down to your right. The track soon levels out and leads straight on through woodland for a further 0.25 miles then, where the stone wall ends on your right, head right through a gate in this wall (waymarker post on the left-side of the track - SE 141 685). Follow the clear grassy track slanting down across the hillside to reach the dam wall of Gouthwaite Reservoir. Head through the wrought-iron gate beside the dam wall and follow the path down through woodland then straight on across rough fields, with the wooded banks of the River Nidd just to your right, to reach the road beside the narrow Wath Bridge (SE 144 677) - *Sportsman's Arms short detour to the left.*

At the road, take the footpath directly opposite (signpost 'Pateley Bridge'), over a footbridge across Black Dike stream then head straight on across the field to reach a squeeze-stile. After the squeeze-stile, carry straight on bearing slightly to the left across the next field to join the raised grassy track-bed of the former Nidd Valley Light Railway. Follow this old track-bed straight on across fields over stiles and through gates then passing a large pond on your left below Low Green House beyond which the old track-bed joins the wooded banks of the River Nidd (SE 151 667). Continue straight on along the clear riverside path all the way to Pateley Bridge. As you approach the outskirts of the town you pass the new Millennium Bridge (footbridge) across the river and then a weir just after which you reach the houses on the edge of Pateley Bridge. Do not head along the road into the housing estate but carry straight on along the enclosed path passing to the right behind the houses to join the bottom of Mill Lane beside some old stone-built houses. Follow this lane straight on to reach the bridge at the foot of the High Street in the centre of Pateley Bridge (SE 157 655).

MAP FOUR

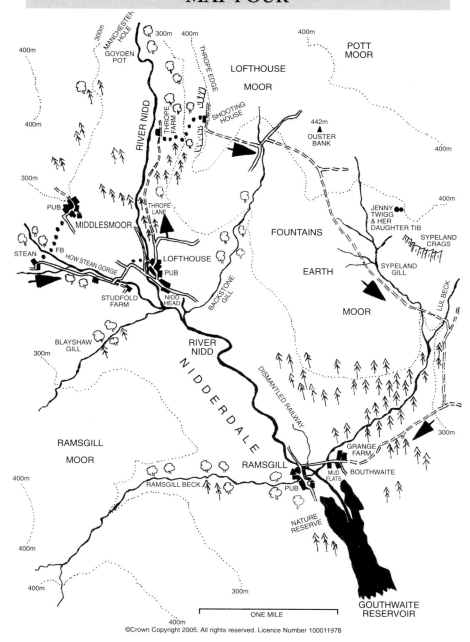

MANCHESTER HOLE

300m 400m

GOYDEN POT

THROPE EDGE

LOFTHOUSE

MOOR

POTT MOOR

400m

400m

THROPE FARM

SHOOTING HOUSE

442m
OUSTER BANK

400m

RIVER NIDD

400m

300m

PUB

MIDDLESMOOR

THROPE LANE

JENNY TWIGG & HER DAUGHTER TIB

400m

FOUNTAINS

SYPELAND CRAGS

STEAN

FB

HOW STEAN GORGE

LOFTHOUSE

PUB

EARTH

SYPELAND GILL

STUDFOLD FARM

NIDD HEAD

BACKSTONE GILL

MOOR

LUL BECK

BLAYSHAW GILL

300m

RIVER NIDD

DISMANTLED RAILWAY

N I D D E R D A L E

RAMSGILL MOOR

400m

RAMSGILL BECK

RAMSGILL

GRANGE FARM

MUD FLATS

BOUTHWAITE

300m

PUB

NATURE RESERVE

400m

400m

300m

GOUTHWAITE RESERVOIR

ONE MILE

400m

©Crown Copyright 2005. All rights reserved. Licence Number 100011978

36

MAP FIVE

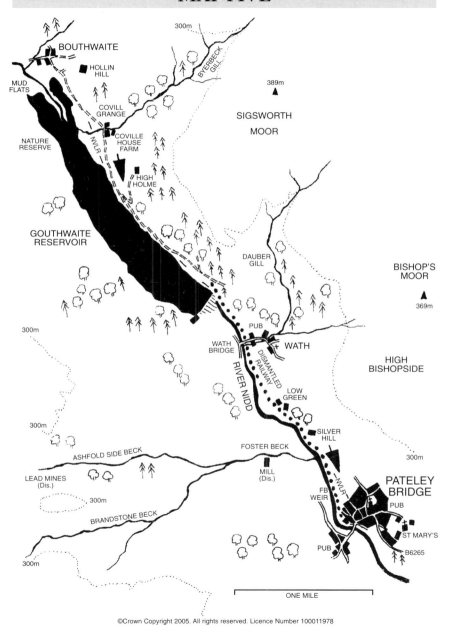

BOUTHWAITE

HOLLIN HILL

MUD FLATS

300m

BYERBECK GILL

389m ▲

SIGSWORTH MOOR

COVILL GRANGE

NATURE RESERVE

NVLR

COVILLE HOUSE FARM

HIGH HOLME

GOUTHWAITE RESERVOIR

DAUBER GILL

BISHOP'S MOOR

369m ▲

300m

PUB

WATH BRIDGE

WATH

HIGH BISHOPSIDE

RIVER NIDD

DISMANTLED RAILWAY

LOW GREEN

300m

SILVER HILL

ASHFOLD SIDE BECK

FOSTER BECK

300m

LEAD MINES (Dis.)

300m

MILL (Dis.)

FB WEIR

NVLR

PATELEY BRIDGE

PUB

BRANDSTONE BECK

PUB

ST MARY'S

B6265

300m

ONE MILE

37

POINTS OF INTEREST

HOW STEAN GORGE

How Stean Beck is born on the flanks of Meugher (575 metres), one of the most remote fells in the Yorkshire Dales that rises up above a vast tract of moorland between Nidderdale and Wharfedale. The waters tumble down through a narrow ravine across these moors before reaching the gentler fields and wooded gills around the hamlet of Stean; however, the stream shows its wild side one last time before it swells the waters of the River Nidd near Lofthouse. For over half a mile, How Stean Beck flows through a narrow limestone ravine known as How Stean Gorge. Over thousands of years, the tumbling waters have eroded down through the bed of limestone to create 'The Little Switzerland of England'. The gorge is up to 80-ft deep in places with rocks ledges, cliffs, draping ferns and overhanging trees. Part of the walk around the gorge includes a subterranean trip through Tom Taylor's Cave, a 530-ft underground cavern. Roman coins were found in this cave, which is named after a local highwayman who used it as his hideout.

LOFTHOUSE

Lofthouse is a delightful village situated at the junction with the steep moorland road that leads up across Pott Moor over to the old market town of Masham. In the 12th Century, much of Upper Nidderdale was owned by Roger de Mowbray, who also founded Byland Abbey near Helmsley and subsequently granted grazing lands to the monks on the western side of the valley. He later sold land on the east side of the valley to Fountains Abbey, who established a grange (monastic farm) at Lofthouse around which the village grew. The oldest part of the village is grouped around the foot of the steep moorland road, a compact cluster of grey-stone cottages and farms with a small 'square' of houses overlooking the Memorial Water Fountain. This water fountain was built in 1920 to commemorate the local men who gave their lives during the Great War and features some rather amusing inscriptions including:
A pint of cold water three times a day
is the surest way to keep doctor away.

If you want to be healthy, wealthy and stout
Use plenty of cold water inside and out.

There are a number of other water fountains throughout the village including one built in 1918 to commemorate the signing of the Armistice, a rare dedication. More modern houses line the main valley road around its junction with the moorland road including a row of Waterworks Cottages and the former station along the Nidd Valley Light Railway (NVLR). This railway was operated by Bradford Corporation during the construction of Scar House and Angram reservoirs to supply these two remote reservoir sites with goods and materials. Uniquely, they also ran a passenger service from Pateley Bridge up through Nidderdale as far as Lofthouse, beyond which only freight trains continued up to the reservoirs. The railway closed in 1936.

RIVER NIDD
Between Scar House Reservoir and Lofthouse the River Nidd flows through a dramatic steep-sided valley. This is Upper Nidderdale, a starkly beautiful landscape of steep bracken-covered slopes, woodland copse, isolated farmsteads and undulating fields of rich green criss-crossed by drystone walls all of which is hemmed in by gritstone edges and heather moorland. The riverbed along this stretch of the valley is composed of limestone rock as opposed to the millstone grit that is more commonly found throughout Nidderdale. Over many thousands of years, water has percolated down through the many fissures and faults in the limestone bedrock and has gradually dissolved the rock to create an underground labyrinth of caves and passages. Indeed, the river sinks into a pothole at the foot of Beggarmoat Scar some two miles north of Lofthouse near Manchester Hole, a cave entrance that leads down into the main underground river channel which soon links up with the complex and dangerous cave system of Goyden Pot. For over two miles the River Nidd follows a subterranean route through caves and passageways before reappearing just to the south of Lofthouse at Nidd Heads. Only after heavy rain does the river flow over-ground; indeed the popular caving routes of Manchester Hole and Goyden Pot are often subject to sudden and severe flooding when the river spills through the

normally dry cave entrance of Manchester Hole; these caves should only be tackled by experts. From Lofthouse, the old farm track of Thrope Lane heads up through this valley across steep wooded slopes. From the old farmhouse of Thrope Farm, a bridleway leads steeply up across birchwood slopes onto the gritstone escarpment of Thrope Edge beside a conspicuous castellated shooting house that looks rather like a church when viewed from below. The views from Thrope Edge are breath-taking with Upper Nidderdale falling steeply away below your feet and the massive bulk of the Great Whernside ridge on the horizon.

FOUNTAINS EARTH MOOR

Fountains Earth Moor forms a vast expanse of heather moorland between Upper Nidderdale and lower Wensleydale stretching in all directions as far as the eye can see, gently rising and falling like a huge billowing blanket. There is a stark beauty in landscape such as this; wild, remote and desolate yet at the same time soothing, open and rolling. In spring, acrobatic lapwings dance and dive around these high moors whilst an occasional solitary curlew takes flight soaring across the heather. In medieval times this moorland was used by the monks of nearby Fountains Abbey as grazing land for their flocks of sheep, controlled through their granges at Lofthouse, Bouthwaite and Covill. Founded in 1132, Fountains Abbey quickly grew to become one of Europe's richest and most powerful religious houses with large-scale farming, mining, smelting, quarrying and horse breeding interests. The most important development for Fountains was the introduction of the Cistercian system of lay brothers. These men were an integral part of the Abbey and served as masons, tanners and smiths, although their main job was to look after the sheep flocks, which grazed their huge estate that stretched across the North of England. All this came to an abrupt end in 1539 with Henry VIII's Dissolution of the Monasteries. Today, the remains of Fountains Abbey are an outstanding example of Cistercian life and architecture and are protected as a World Heritage Site.

Fountains Earth Moor is criss-crossed by several old County Roads, technically public highways, which were once important routes across the moors to Masham, Kirkby Malzeard, Ripon and Fountains Abbey. An old road leads steadily down alongside the moorland stream of

Sypeland Gill with the impressive outcrops of Sypeland Crags across to your left. Two weathered outcrops stand out, conspicuous against the skyline, known as Jenny Twigg and her Daughter Tib. Who they are named after no-one really knows, although it is possible that the names date back to the days of superstition, folklore and witchcraft. The name Jennet (and other closely related names including Jenny) was often associated with witches in medieval times. Perhaps Jenny and Tib were witches turned to stone on the moors! The old road leads down over a large stone bridge across Lul Beck then skirts above forest to join the old monastic route from Bouthwaite to Fountains Abbey, which we follow steeply down to reach this hamlet. This descent is superb with a 'surprise view' as the mudflats and shallow reed-filled waters at the head of Gouthwaite Reservoir come into view.

BOUTHWAITE

Bouthwaite is a small hamlet that lies hidden away from the main valley road beside the wooded stream of Lul Beck. This was the site of a grange of Fountains Abbey; indeed the beautiful old stone farmhouse of Bouthwaite Grange, dated 1673, probably stands on the site of this original grange. Bouthwaite and neighbouring Ramsgill across the River Nidd were once served by a station along the NVLR, which can still be seen alongside the road towards Ramsgill.

RAMSGILL

Ramsgill, its feet dipping into the mudflats at the northern end of Gouthwaite Reservoir, is perhaps the prettiest village in Nidderdale with old stone houses looking out across an attractive green that is divided in two by Ramsgill Beck. Dominating the village is the ivy-clad Yorke Arms Hotel, one-time shooting lodge of the Yorke family who lived at Gouthwaite Hall before it was demolished to make way for the reservoir. It is now a rather elegant hotel and bar renowned for the quality of its food - a 'restaurant with rooms', as it says on the sign. In medieval times, the village developed around the grange, mill and chapel of Byland Abbey; the remains of one of the gables of this monastic chapel can still be seen near to the present Victorian church which was built in 1842. Following the Dissolution of the Monasteries, Henry VIII sold off the Crown's newly acquired monastic lands in Nidderdale to the Yorke family.

GOUTHWAITE RESERVOIR

Gouthwaite Reservoir was completed in 1901, the first of a trio of huge reservoirs that flooded large tracts of Upper Nidderdale to provide drinking water for the burgeoning industrial city of Bradford. Gouthwaite was built as a compensation reservoir for the larger supply reservoirs of Angram and Scar House at the head of the valley. This role as a compensation reservoir means that water levels fluctuate regularly as water is released to maintain the flow of the River Nidd, originally to provide water power for the many mills that once stood alongside the river although the releases are now predominantly made to meet environmental demands. During the 19th Century there were at least forty mills along the banks of the Nidd between Pateley Bridge and Knaresborough processing flax, corn, rope, and cotton - Nidderdale was once famous for its linen weaving. By the 1960s most of these mills had closed. A rather curious legacy of the age of water power is that the water releases from Gouthwaite are not controlled by Yorkshire Water but by the Gouthwaite Reservoir Board, an independent committee that was formed to protect the water flow and power needs of the local business community. The Gouthwaite Reservoir Board is still going today, despite the closure of the watermills.

The stone-built dam is impressive with a series of large arches spanning the dam wall surmounted by castellated towers. To maintain the flow of the Nidd, a powerful force of water thunders from two outlet chutes at the base of the dam wall and, if you are fortunate enough to visit after heavy rain, water also cascades over the dam wall sending a foaming torrent spilling down the rough stone-work. Of the three Nidderdale reservoirs, Gouthwaite looks the most natural with nature reserves along its banks and expansive mudflats at its northern end that attract a great number of breeding wildfowl, waders, birds of prey as well as migratory birds; over 200 species have been recorded. The former track-bed of the NVLR can also be seen along the eastern banks of the reservoir.

WATH

Wath is a delightful hamlet of old stone cottages and farms set amongst wooded slopes and sylvan pastures. Here you will also find the Sportsman's Arms, a fine country restaurant and hotel with an excellent reputation for food. Across the road from the Sportsman's Arms is the former Wath Station along the NVLR. Wath is also home to one of the two smallest Methodist chapels in the country, a unique five-sided chapel that was built in the 1850s at the end of a row of cottages. Inside, a gallery cleverly makes use of the limited space, so much so that it can seat 50 people! Rudyard Kipling's father frequently preached in this chapel, which is still in regular use. The village is reached across a narrow packhorse bridge across the River Nidd that was originally built by the monks of Fountains Abbey to reach their grange at Bewerley near Pateley Bridge; 'wath' is the Old Norse word for a ford.

Sportsmans Arms, Wath

PATELEY BRIDGE
Pateley Bridge is the 'capital of Nidderdale', a lovely old town of gritstone houses lining a steep High Street with many hidden side-streets for you to explore leisurely on foot where you will find a theatre, museum, historic ruined church, England's oldest sweet shop established in 1827 and an ancient bridge. There has been a river crossing at Pateley Bridge for possibly 2,000 years as it is thought that the Romans came this way to their lead mines on the moors around Greenhow. A bridge

was first recorded in 1320, before which there was a ford across the river. Pateley Bridge grew in importance as it lay on the busy monastic road from Fountains Abbey over to Wharfedale as well as the old High Road to Craven. In the 18th and 19th centuries a number of turnpike roads were established which, coupled with the local mines, quarries and mills, meant that the town soon became a bustling place. At weekends the navvies who had worked all week on the dams came into town for a drink along with the local quarrymen, miners and mill-workers - by all accounts it was like the Wild West! By the end of the 19th Century, Pateley Bridge supported two breweries and several pubs, most of which have now closed; indeed a closer look as you walk up the steep narrow High Street will reveal a number of old coaching inns and taverns. 'The Nidderdale Brewery, J Metcalfe & Sons', first established in 1775, grew to become a large commercial brewer until it closed in 1912 - the brewery stood at the top of the High Street where the gardens are today. Pateley's other brewery was located in Bridgehousegate across the ancient bridge over the River Nidd, which was founded by a Metcalfe after a family row. This old brewery can still be seen and stands as a wonderful example of a Victorian 'tower brewery' - ingredients go in at the top (water, malt, hops, yeast) and beer comes out at the bottom!

Tucked away off the High Street along Church Street is The Playhouse, which is housed in a Primitive Methodist Chapel built in 1859, whilst nearby along King Street is the award-winning Nidderdale Museum, housed in the former Victorian workhouse. This imposing building with its two protruding gable ends was built in 1863 to provide shelter for the needy of the area; however it closed in 1914 although the Vagrant Ward continued to be used until the Second World War. Just beyond Millfield Street is the former station of the NVLR, which was operated by Bradford Corporation between 1907 and 1936 to service the construction of the two huge dams in upper Nidderdale and also provided a passenger service as far as Lofthouse. This railway crossed the bottom of the High Street by way of a level crossing and then met up with the North Eastern Railway branch line from the Harrogate to Ripon line. This NER railway opened in 1862 although passenger services were withdrawn in 1951 and the branch line closed completely in 1964. The old NER station building still stands along Nidd Walk - remarkably, Pateley Bridge once had two stations!

From the top of the steep High Street just beyond the Methodist Church a flagged path known as the Panorama Walk leads quite steeply up to reach the forlorn ruins of St Mary's Church. Unbelievably, this path was the main road between Pateley Bridge and Fountains Abbey in medieval times. This lovely old church, now a roofless ruin, dates from the late 13th Century, with later additions during the 17th Century including the tower in 1691. The Church was abandoned in the early 19th Century due to its inconvenient location up a steep hill away from the developing town beside the river crossing. This area is known as Church Green and was probably the site of the original settlement, indeed the name of the town is derived from the Anglo-Saxon word 'patleia' meaning a 'path through a clearing'. A new church dedicated to St Cuthbert was built in the town in 1828 to replace St Mary's Church.

Gouthwaite Reservoir

STAGE THREE
- Pateley Bridge to Ilkley -

WALK INFORMATION

Highlights   Bewerley Grange Chapel, great views from the Two Stoops, a wonderful gritstone escarpment, the monk's bridge, the flooded village of West End, Washburn's rapids, by the banks of Fewston and Swinsty, overlooking Wharfedale, the leader of the New Model Army and the heather spa.

Distance		
Pateley Bridge to Blubberhouses	9 miles	
Blubberhouses to Ilkley	9.5 miles	
Total	18.5 miles *	

Time   8 - 9 hours

Grid References   Grid References have been given to assist route finding; for example the Grid Reference for Yorke's Folly is SE 157 635

Refreshments   Pubs at Pateley Bridge, Thruscross, Blubberhouses and Ilkley. Cafés and shops at Pateley Bridge and Ilkley. Timble Inn closed at time of writing.

Terrain   From Pateley Bridge, a quiet lane leads through Bewerley before field and moorland paths climb up to reach Yorke's Folly. A moorland path then heads across Guisecliff to join a stony track beside a TV mast, which is followed all the way to Heyshaw. Quiet country lanes, field paths and farm tracks then lead to Thornthwaite and up to join the Greenhow Hill Road near the Stone House Inn. From here, a lane heads down to reach the dam wall of Thruscross Reservoir from where a path slants down across the hillside to join a track that soon leads onto a wooded riverside path which is followed down to the A59 at Blubberhouses. A clear path then heads along the shores of Fewston and Swinsty reservoirs before a path strikes off through forest then across fields to Timble. After a short stretch of road walking, a track heads off across Denton Moor to reach Ellarcarr Pike from where a rough path leads steadily down across open moorland, to join the top of a lane that leads down into Denton. Quiet lanes and field paths are then followed into Ilkley.

Ascents	Guisecliff - 310 metres above sea level
	Denton Moor - 290 metres above sea level

Caution   Take extra care along the path across Guisecliff as there are sheer drops and hidden crevices - keep to the path at all times. The River Washburn between Thruscross and Fewston reservoirs is subject to sudden changes in water flow. Take care when crossing the A59 at Blubberhouses. The path across Denton Moor is boggy in places. This walk involves some short sections of road walking along quiet country lanes - take care on these sections, particularly the final stretch as you approach Ilkley.

2-day walk   If you wish, you can divide this Stage Three walk over two days by staying overnight at Blubberhouses. See page 14 for further details.

PUBS ALONG THE WALK

Crown Inn, Pateley Bridge:	01423 712455
Royal Oak, Pateley Bridge:	01423 711577
Harefield Hall Hotel, Pateley Bridge	01423 711429
Stone House Inn, Thruscross	01943 880325
Hopper Lane Hotel, Blubberhouses	01943 880246
Timble Inn, Timble	*Closed at the time of writing*
Several pubs to choose from at Ilkley	*Call Ilkley T.I.C. for details*

FACILITIES ALONG THE WALK

Pateley Bridge	Inn / B&B / Shop / P.O. / Café / Bus / Phone / Toilets / Camp
Bewerley	Phone
Thornthwaite	Phone
Thruscross	Inn / Phone
Blubberhouses	Inn / B&B / Bus / Phone
Swinsty Reservoir	Toilets
Timble	Phone
Denton	Phone
Ilkley	Inn / B&B / Shop / P.O. / Café / Bus / Phone / Toilets / Train

Bewerley Grange Chapel

ROUTE DESCRIPTION

(Map Six)

From the bottom of the High Street in Pateley Bridge, cross the bridge over the River Nidd and follow the road straight on along the B6265 towards 'Grassington' passing the Recreation Ground on your right then, as the road begins to climb uphill, take the road turning to the left opposite the Royal Oak and follow this into Bewerley. Walk through the village passing the 'green' on your left then Bewerley Grange Chapel and continue down along the road out of the village to reach the road bridge across Fosse Gill (SE 158 645). After the bridge, follow the road to the right (SP 'Otley') gently rising up passing the entrance to Skrikes Farm and bending steeply up to the left then, at the top of this bend, cross the wall stile to the right (SP 'Nought Road'). Head straight up the hillside along the grassy path to reach a stile set in a wall at the foot of a wooded bank (Skrikes Wood). Cross the stile and follow the wide path bearing up to the right through the woods then, as you emerge from the woods, the path divides - follow the left-hand path heading up across the heather moorland winding up to soon reach a bridlegate in a wall. Head through the bridlegate and follow the path straight on up across the heather moorland to join Nought Road on a sharp bend (SE 156 636). Cross the road and take the path opposite (SP 'Guisecliff') that leads up bearing very slightly to the left across heather moorland to reach the stone pillars of Yorke's Folly (SE 157 635).

Cross the ladder stile over the wall to your right just after Yorke's Folly, after which turn left along the clear path heading up across the boulder-strewn moorland, with the stone wall just to your left and open moorland stretching away to your right. The path soon re-joins the wall - carry straight on along the clear path alongside this wall heading along the top of the wooded escarpment for 0.5 miles to reach a ladder stile over a fence across your path that leads onto the rocky outcrops of Guisecliff *. *(Warning - extreme care must be taken along this path as there are hidden crevices and sheer drops. Keep well away from the edge and stick to the path).* Follow the path along the top of this rocky escarpment high above Guisecliff Wood all the way to reach the conspicuous TV mast. As you approach the TV mast you reach the end of an old wall - follow the path alongside this wall (with the wall on your left), over a stile then skirt to the right around the TV mast buildings to join a rough track just beyond the buildings (SE 170 631).

The path along the top of Guisecliff is not a legal Right of Way, although is waymarked and well trodden and (at the time of writing) offers an alternative route with good views. The Right of Way as shown on the OS map bears away from the wall at Grid Ref SE 164 633 then heads across the heather moorland to join a rough track just to the right of the TV mast (SE 170 631). At the time of writing there was no sign of this Right of Way on the ground.

Head left along the rough track for a few paces to quickly join a clearer stony track (with the TV mast buildings to your left), marked by a signpost 'Nidderdale Way'. Turn right along this stony track, with the stone wall on your left, and follow it straight on passing High Hood Gap farm then on to reach a gate across your path beside the next farmhouse of Hill Top (SE 172 623). Continue straight on along the track down to reach a road in the hamlet of Heyshaw (SE 173 618).

Turn right up along the road and follow this out of Heyshaw up to reach a T-junction. Turn left down along the road (Dike Lane) for 0.25 miles to reach Dike Lane Head Farm on your right (SE 169 613). Turn right through a wall-gap immediately after the stone barn on your right (before the farmhouse) and walk through the farmyard following the track as it bends round to the left then, immediately before the stone barn on your right just before a T-junction with another track, head right to quickly reach a squeeze-stile tucked away in the corner beside the barn. Cross the stile to quickly join a farm track just beyond the barn, which you follow to the right down to reach Grange House Farm (SE 167 612). As you reach the farm buildings the track forks - follow the left-hand track into the farmyard in front of the farmhouse where you turn left through a metal gate in a fence. Head straight down across the middle of the field to reach a bridle-gate in the wall at the bottom of the field just beyond a small stream (stone slab FB). After the bridle-gate, head to the right alongside the wall on your right and over a wall stile in the field corner, then bear left across the next field and through a gate in a wall (just to the left of the telegraph pole in the wall). After the gate, head straight on alongside the wall on your right to reach Banger House Farm (SE 165 605). Follow the wall passing the farm buildings on your right immediately after which cross the wall-stile beside the gate to your right that leads into a field in front of the farmhouse. After the gate, turn left down across the field passing a telegraph pole in the middle of the field to reach a wall-stile towards the bottom right corner. After this stile, continue straight on alongside the field boundary on your right then, as you reach the bottom of the field (White House Farm in front of you), head to the left to reach a gate that leads onto a track beside the farm *(this short section of permissive path between the field and track avoids the farm gardens)*. Follow the track straight on for a few paces then turn left along a FP immediately before the stone building on your left and follow the path down over a stream then carry on with the stream on your right through woodland to soon join the farm lane beside a bridge. Turn left along this farm lane, over a cattle grid and curving round to the left then, where the lane bends more distinctly to the left (passing place on this bend), head straight on off the track (on this bend) heading up across the rough boulder-strewn hillside to reach a wall corner. Head straight on with the wall on your left through a gate then on to reach a wall stile in the field corner that leads onto a road (SE 169 598). Turn right down the road for a short distance then left over a wall stile (SP 'Thornthwaite Church') and follow the path keeping close to the wall on your left straight on through woodland with Padside Beck just down to your right for 0.5 miles over a series of wall stiles to reach the Packhorse Bridge across the stream, which you cross up to join the road just below Thornthwaite Church (SE 174 594).

(Map Seven)
Turn right up along the road and follow it up passing Thornthwaite Church then bending round to the right around some cottages and carry on along the road winding up to reach a T-junction (SE 171 589). Turn left towards 'Darley, Dacre' and follow this road for about 300 yards then take the road turning to the right towards 'Greenhow Hill'. Follow this road climbing up (My Love Lane) then, just before the road begins to level out, take the walled track to the right (SP 'Greenhow Hill Road')

and follow this straight on to reach a gate at the end of the walled track. After the gate, head straight on bearing slightly to the left up across the rough moorland, over a tumbledown wall then on across the gently rising moorland passing about 100 yards to the left of the outcrops of Calf Crags to reach the bottom of a wall corner. Cross the wall-stile just to the left of this wall corner, after which head diagonally to the left across the rough field (heading towards the left side of the whitewashed Stone House Inn ahead) to reach a metal gate in the corner of the field. Head through the gate and walk straight on alongside the wall on your right to reach Greenhow Hill Road (SE 163 585). Turn right along the road to reach the crossroads beside the Stone House Inn where you turn left along Reservoir Road. Follow this road down to reach the dam wall of Thruscross Reservoir (SE 155 575).

Follow the road across the dam wall, immediately after which take the path to the left down some steps and follow this (SP 'Washburn Valley Path') straight on down across the steep wooded hillside to reach the end of a metalled lane. Turn right along this lane and follow it gently rising up at first before levelling out then carry on along this lane heading down the valley for a further 300 yards until you reach a stony track to your left (that leads back on yourself). Turn left along this track for a few paces then right (after the gate) along a rough grassy track that leads down to a FB across the River Washburn (SE 157 568). After the FB turn right along the track - follow this clear riverside path alongside the meandering River Washburn heading downstream for 1.25 miles (keep to the riverside path all the way) to reach the A59 at Blubberhouses beside the road-bridge (SE 168 553). *Hopper Lane Hotel 0.5 miles to left along A59 towards Harrogate at top of the steep hill.*

Turn right along the A59 for a few paces and cross the road (take care) by the road turning towards 'Otley' below the small church then turn immediately left through the parking area for Fewston Reservoir to reach a gate at the far end beside the head of the reservoir. Head through the gate and follow the stony path straight on for 1.75 miles along the meandering wooded shoreline of Fewston Reservoir all the way to reach a road junction opposite the entrance to Swinsty Reservoir car park (dam wall of Fewston Reservoir just down to your left - SE 186 538).

Cross the road then turn left along the walled stony track just by the car park entrance and toilet block (Yorkshire Water 'Swinsty Reservoir' sign and 'Public Footpath' signpost). Follow this walled track straight on down through woodland to join the wooded banks of Swinsty Reservoir then take the track to the right ('Permissive Path' sign) immediately before the walled gardens of Swinsty Hall (SE 194 533). Follow this track up to reach a gate beside the entrance to the Hall. Head through the gate and follow the path curving round to the right through woodland for a short distance then, where the track straightens out, turn left back on yourself along a footpath. Follow this path straight on through the woods (Swinsty Hall across to your left) to join a rough track and tumbledown wall across your path. Turn right up along this track to reach a gate at the top of the woods (SE 191 531). Head through the gate then walk straight on up across three fields through a series of gates to join the bottom of a walled grassy track which you follow up to join a lane on the outskirts of Timble. Follow this lane to the right to emerge into a small 'square' at the top end of the village (SE 179 529).

Walk across the 'square' to quickly join the main road through the village and follow this to the left up out of Timble. Continue straight on along this road leaving the village behind for just over 0.25 miles to reach a T-junction where you head left to soon reach a crossroads beside Lane End Farm (SE 170 531). Cross the road (take care) and follow the stony lane opposite up passing some houses and then Sourby Old Farm on your left and continue along the stony track to join the edge of a large plantation on your right. Carry straight on along the track with the plantation on your right for a further 150 yards then, where the track forks ('no vehicles' sign), follow the track to the left (away from the plantation) to reach a gate and cattle grid on the edge of open moorland (SE 164 527). Cross the cattle grid and follow the clear track bending round to the right then climbing gradually up across the moorland to reach two gates on the 'rise' of Ellarcarr Pike (with Ellarcarr Farm just down to your right - SE 159 523).

(Map Eight)
Head over the stile beside the left-hand gate (ignore the gate to the right towards Ellarcarr Farm) and follow the wide path straight on across the

heather moorland to soon join a fence on your left. Carry straight on alongside this fence on your left (ignore any stiles over this fence) heading gradually down across Denton Moor for 0.75 miles. As you approach the bottom of the moorland you pass to the right of a small plantation, at which point follow the grassy path bearing slightly to the right away from the fence, over a ford across Lady Dikes (stream) to reach a metal gate/bridlegate beside the bottom left corner of a long narrow belt of woodland at the bottom of Denton Moor (Moor Plantation - SE 151 513). Head through the gate and walk straight on alongside the wall on your left, through a gate in a fence across your path then carry straight on (wall on your left) heading gradually down the hillside (Ilkley Moor and lower Wharfedale ahead) to reach a gate through the wall to your left in the bottom corner of the field. Head through the gate and turn right heading down across the hillside with the wall now on your right (path becomes a grassy track) down to reach a cattle grid at the top of a walled lane just to the left of Yarnett House Farm (SE 149 502). Cross the cattle grid and follow the lane (Smithy Lane) straight on for 1 mile down to reach the village of Denton (SE 144 490).

As you reach the road junction in the centre of the village (beside the red 'phone box) turn right for a short distance then left at the triangular green (with the lamppost and circular stone Fountain) and follow this down out of Denton. Where the road bends to the left, turn right through a gate along a track (SE 143 486). Follow this track straight on across a field to join the bottom corner of West Park Wood on your right - carry straight on alongside this woodland then, where the track bends to the right through a double gate into woodland, head straight on (do not enter the woodland) to quickly reach a stile beside a gate in the field corner. Cross the stile and continue straight on alongside the fence / woodland over another stile beside a gate, after which carry on for a further 25 yards then, where the fence / woodland bends to the right, head straight on across the field to reach a small metal gate near the farm buildings of Beck Foot Farm (SE 135 486). Head through the gate and walk straight on into farmyard and follow the farm track to the right passing in front of the farmhouse, over a bridge across Bow Beck and on to reach the road. At the road, take the path opposite (SP) through a wooden kissing gate (ignore the metal gate and track) out onto a field. Walk straight on alongside the overgrown hedge on your right across the field to reach a stile, after which walk bear left across the middle of the field to reach a stile towards the far left corner that leads onto Denton Road (SE 129 484). Turn right along the road (take care) for 0.3 miles then cross the suspension bridge to your left over the River Wharfe (SE 123 485). After the bridge, follow the clear riverside path to the right for 0.5 miles all the way to reach the road bridge over the Wharfe (New Bridge). Head up the steps onto the bridge and turn left into the centre of Ilkley.

Thornthwaite Packhorse Bridge

MAP SIX

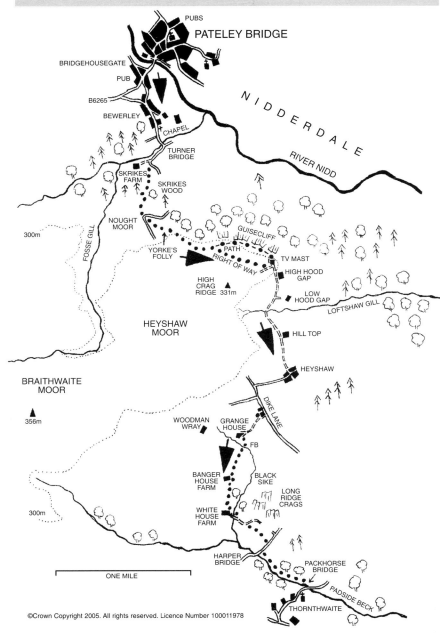

PUBS

PATELEY BRIDGE

BRIDGEHOUSEGATE

PUB

B6265

BEWERLEY

CHAPEL

TURNER
BRIDGE

SKRIKES
FARM

SKRIKES
WOOD

NOUGHT
MOOR

FOSSE GILL

300m

YORKE'S
FOLLY

GUISECLIFF

PATH
RIGHT OF WAY

TV MAST

HIGH HOOD
GAP

HIGH
CRAG
RIDGE 331m

LOW
HOOD GAP

LOFTSHAW GILL

HEYSHAW
MOOR

HILL TOP

HEYSHAW

BRAITHWAITE
MOOR

DIKE LANE

356m

WOODMAN
WRAY

GRANGE
HOUSE

FB

BANGER
HOUSE
FARM

BLACK
SIKE

LONG
RIDGE
CRAGS

300m

WHITE
HOUSE
FARM

HARPER
BRIDGE

PACKHORSE
BRIDGE

ONE MILE

PADSIDE BECK

THORNTHWAITE

N I D D E R D A L E

RIVER NIDD

56

MAP SEVEN

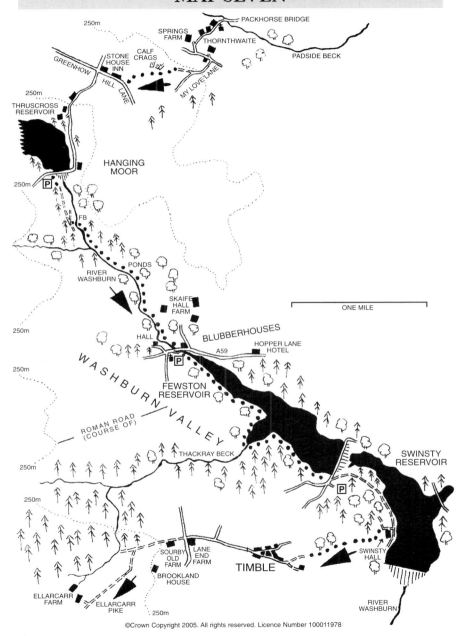

250m

PACKHORSE BRIDGE

SPRINGS
FARM

THORNTHWAITE

CALF
CRAGS

STONE
HOUSE
INN

GREENHOW

HILL LANE

PADSIDE BECK

MY LOVE LANE

250m

THRUSCROSS
RESERVOIR

HANGING
MOOR

250m P

FB

RIVER
WASHBURN

PONDS

SKAIFE
HALL
FARM

ONE MILE

250m

HALL

BLUBBERHOUSES

A59

HOPPER LANE
HOTEL

250m P

FEWSTON
RESERVOIR

WASHBURN VALLEY

ROMAN ROAD
(COURSE OF)

THACKRAY BECK

SWINSTY
RESERVOIR

250m

250m P

250m

SOURBY
OLD
FARM

LANE
END
FARM

TIMBLE

SWINSTY
HALL

BROOKLAND
HOUSE

ELLARCARR
FARM

ELLARCARR
PIKE

250m

RIVER
WASHBURN

57

MAP EIGHT

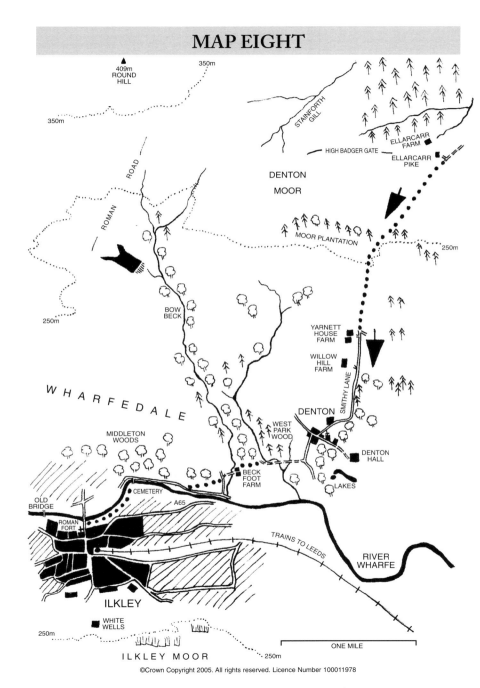

58

POINTS OF INTEREST

BEWERLEY

Bewerley lies just across the river from Pateley Bridge, a delightful village of attractive cottages facing onto a small green complete with a red 'phone box, mature trees and an old water trough still with a working tap. Bewerley was first mentioned in the Domesday Book, making it much older than Pateley Bridge. In the 12th Century Roger de Mowbray, lord of the Manor, granted the monks of Fountains Abbey land around Bewerley where they subsequently developed an important sheep and cattle grange. These granges included a farm, dairy, hall, dormitory and chapel from where the monks would administer and manage their lands and livestock, although the manual work was done by lay brothers. Hidden away along the road through the village is Bewerley Grange Chapel, built between 1494 and 1526 by Marmaduke Huby, one of the last Abbots of Fountains Abbey before the Dissolution of the Monasteries by Henry VIII. On the far gable end of this simple chapel is a carved inscription "Soli Deo Honor Et Gloria" that translates as "Glory and Honour be to God alone" with the initials M.H. - this was the motto of Abbot Huby, which can also be found inscribed on the side of the Tower at Fountains Abbey. The appearance of the chapel has changed little since it was built.

YORKE'S FOLLY

Visible for miles around, the conspicuous landmark of Yorke's Folly was built in around 1810 by John Yorke of Bewerley Hall to provide employment for his labourers during a period of hardship and economic depression; the labourers were paid one shilling a day plus a loaf of bread. There were originally three pillars when it was known as the Three Stoops, however, one fell down during a storm in 1893 since when it has been known as the Two Stoops! Inspected at close quarters, the pillars have an almost ecclesiastical feel about them as if they originally came from the nave of some great church. The view from the Folly is superb with Upper Nidderdale stretching away into the distance.

GUISECLIFF

Guisecliff is an abrupt escarpment of weathered sandstone that juts out high above Guisecliff Woods with sheer drops and hidden crevices. These weathered rocks are formed from the same gritstone deposits as the more famous Brimham Rocks, which can be seen across the valley. They were formed some 300 million years ago when great rivers flowed over this landscape depositing sand and mud which, over time, were compressed to form sedimentary rocks known as millstone grit. These rocks were exposed to the elements following the last Ice Age since when, over thousands of years, they have been ravaged by frost, ice, wind and water creating the rock masses and tors we see today. The views from this escarpment are breath-taking with Nidderdale laid out before you and Gouthwaite Reservoir sparkling in the distance.

THORNTHWAITE

In medieval times, the scattered hamlet of Thornthwaite stood on the edge of the Royal Forest of Knaresborough, a vast swathe of land bounded by the rivers Nidd, Washburn and Wharfe that stretched all the way beyond Knaresborough towards the Vale of York. This was a Royal hunting preserve owned by the Duchy of Lancaster and administered from Knaresborough Castle where many Kings of England came to hunt wild boar, wolves and deer; King John was a frequent visitor and John of Gaunt grew up at Knaresborough Castle. A delightful path leads across the gently shelving wooded banks of Padside Beck alongside a stone wall which once marked the boundary of the Forest of Knaresbrough. The path leads past an old cobbled spring complete with drinking troughs, just beyond which is a wonderful old packhorse bridge. This small hump-back bridge was built by the monks travelling between Fountains Abbey and Bolton Priory.

Just above the bridge is St Saviour's Church, a simple church with a lovely setting amongst old yew trees. There has been a chapel on this site since at least 1409, although the present church dates from 1810. Inside the church is a stone tablet from Holy Trinity Church at Thruscross which disappeared beneath the waters of Thruscross Reservoir in 1966. A quiet country road with the delightful name of My Love Lane heads up out of Thornthwaite before a track turns off across moorland passing the gritstone outcrops of Calf Crags. A wonderful view unfolds back across the undulating pastures of Thornthwaite towards the TV mast above Guisecliff. This is a beautiful corner of Nidderdale, a wonderful landscape of scattered farms, drystone walls and heather-clad heights.

THRUSCROSS RESERVOIR

Thruscross Reservoir is the uppermost of the four large reservoirs along the beautiful Washburn Valley which supply water to Leeds; it is also perhaps the most intriguing. When the dam wall was built across the narrow steep-sided valley in 1966 and the peaty waters began to slowly rise, the village of West End gradually disappeared beneath the waves. This was once a thriving village with several mills alongside the fast-flowing River Washburn, Holy Trinity Church, Methodist Chapel, school, an old stone bridge and the Gate Inn. According to the historian Arthur Mee ('Yorkshire, West Riding' 1941), one of these mills had a terrible reputation during Victorian times, *"Here scores of children are said to have been employed by brutal masters who kept them standing at the looms till they fell exhausted."* Perhaps it is better that these old mills have disappeared deep beneath Thruscross Reservoir. When I was much younger I was led to believe that West End village was still standing beneath the reservoir and, if I looked carefully, I might just catch sight of the steeple poking above the surface - images of fish swimming around the pews of the church sprang to mind! This image was shattered somewhat when, in the dry summer of 1990, the water level fell so much that the village re-appeared. I slid down a steep muddy bank, crossed tumbledown walls and walked over the old stone bridge spanning the River Washburn. There were no buildings standing, only piles of stones and lots of tree stumps - the whole of the village had been demolished in 1965 prior to flooding and the churchyard moved to higher ground just off Greenhow Hill Road, although the layout of the lanes and fields could still clearly be seen. Downstream of the impressive concrete dam wall with its 200-metre drop (which, incidentally, holds back 1,725 million gallons of water), the Washburn Valley remains very much intact with thickly wooded banks carpeted by a profusion of wild flowers, flat meadows and the River Washburn tumbling across its rocky bed. Several times a year, water is released from the dam to create a challenging canoe course along the narrow, rocky, meandering riverbed where regular competitions are held including the Wild Water Racing championships. This delightful river landscape lasts for about two miles before the river begins to back up once again at Blubberhouses, trapped behind the dam of Fewston Reservoir.

For a short circular walk around this reservoir:
Thruscross walk (4.5 miles) www.yorkshirewater.com/?OBH=522&ID=795

BLUBBERHOUSES

The humorous name of this hamlet is thought to be derived from the 'houses by the bubbling stream' and is known throughout the country from traffic reports as the A59 at Blubberhouses is often one of the first roads to be closed by snow. The A59 between Harrogate and Skipton is also reputedly the most dangerous road in Britain. This scattered hamlet lies just off the A59 along the Greenhow Hill Road, a handful of cottages, farms and a cricket pitch. The diminutive St Andrew's Church overlooks the parking area beside the head of Fewston Reservoir, built using stones recycled from the old church at Thruscross that disappeared beneath the waters of the reservoir.

FEWSTON & SWINSTY RESERVOIRS

Fewston (1897) and Swinsty (1876) reservoirs are two of the most popular reservoirs in Yorkshire for walking, bird-watching and trout fishing. They both have beautiful settings amongst rolling wooded hills with well-maintained circular paths around their shore-lines from where there are wonderful views across reed-fringed waters; they feel more like natural lakes than reservoirs. The mud banks at the head of Fewston are renowned for wildlife, in particular waders, ducks and geese although you may be lucky enough to catch a glimpse of a buzzard circling above. Yorkshire Water has worked closely in recent years with partners in the Washburn Valley (Nidderdale AONB, Bradford Ornithological Group and the Wharfedale Naturalists Society) to enhance habitats for birds, mammals, amphibians and reptiles. There are now more than twenty pairs of buzzards in the valley. Nightjars as well as long-eared owls have recently returned to the area to breed, and the occasional osprey drops by to feed en route to Scotland and the Lake District. Ponds and clear-felled areas amongst the coniferous plantations have encouraged breeding sites for dragonfly, frogs, newts and toads. Fewston and Swinsty reservoirs, along with Lindley Wood Reservoir (1875) further down the Washburn Valley, were originally built by Leeds Corporation during the late 19th Century; they are still used for the production of water for the Leeds area. Hidden amongst woodland beside the banks of Swinsty Reservoir stands Swinsty Hall, a wonderful example of an Elizabethan hall with a delightfully haphazard layout, lots of gables and mullion windows as well as tall chimney stacks. For centuries the Hall was owned by the Robinson family, one of whom emigrated to New York but never forgot his roots and later founded the Robinson Library and Free School at Timble in 1892. According to travel writer Edmund Bogg ('A 1000 Miles in Wharfedale' 1892), the original builder of the Hall many centuries ago acquired his wealth by travelling to London during an outbreak of the plague and amassed great quantities of gold and silver by robbing the dead victims and stealing from their deserted houses! When he returned to Yorkshire with his loot, the locals shunned him in fear of catching the plague themselves and so he took refuge in a local barn and subsequently built this fine Hall.

For short circular walks around these reservoirs:
Fewston & Timble walk (6.5 miles) www.yorkshirewater.com/?OBH=522&ID=777
Swinsty walk (3 miles) www.yorkshirewater.com/?OBH=522&ID=2060

TIMBLE
The delightful village of Timble is situated on a broad ridge of land overlooking the Washburn Valley with fine views from its south side down along the valley towards Lindley Wood Reservoir. The village boasts attractive stone-built houses and cottages including a handful of 17th Century farms as well as an old water fountain, the Robinson Library and Free School and the former Timble Inn at the heart of the village. This historic and unpretentious Dales pub was a popular haunt of walkers and fishermen but recently closed. The bar remains very much intact - a glimpse of how country pubs used to be half a century ago - and will hopefully re-open soon.

DENTON MOOR
Denton Moor is a large expanse of moorland between Wharfedale and

the Washburn Valley with wonderful views in all directions. On the steady climb up to Ellarcarr Pike there are superb views down towards Lindley Wood Reservoir whilst to the north you can just see the dam wall of Thruscross Reservoir. Many old tracks meet at Ellarcarr Pike including High Badger Gate, an ancient trading route between Ilkley and Ripon - a glance at the OS map will reveal several old County Roads across these moors as well as the old Roman Road that once linked the Roman forts at Ilkley and Aldborough. This moorland is also littered with prehistoric remains including cup and ring marked rocks. No one really knows the true meaning of the cup and ring carvings; they could be fertility symbols, religious carvings or perhaps messages for other people travelling through the area as they are usually located on high ground or beside ancient trackways. The long and steady descent down into Wharfedale is superb with Ilkley sheltering beneath the rugged outcrops and heather moorland of the famous Ilkley Moor.

DENTON

Denton is a peaceful village of attractive cottages sheltered amongst woodland copse overlooking Wharfedale. For such a small place it has a fascinating history for just to the east of the village stands Denton Hall, which was once the home of the Fairfax family. The original Denton Hall was built in the early 16th Century by Sir William Fairfax, however, this Hall was destroyed by fire and subsequently replaced by the present Hall in 1778, designed by the famous architect John Carr. By this time, the estate had been sold to the Ibbetson family of Leeds as Lord Fairfax needed to pay off some debts. The most famous family member was Thomas Fairfax who was born at Denton in 1612. He later became the Parliamentary general of the New Model Army during the English Civil War and defeated Charles I at Naseby, although he was later replaced by Cromwell as he refused to march against the Scots who had proclaimed Charles II as king. Ownership of the Hall has since passed through a number of families and it is currently used as a company headquarters and management training centre. Close to the gates of the Hall stands St Helen's Church, a wonderful example of Georgian architecture with an attractive lantern tower, again designed by John Carr. Inside there is a painted glass 'music' window by Henry Gyles of York, dated 1700 that originally came from the Hall. In the centre of the village set on a small green is a large apple-shaped stone known as the Fountain that once provided the village water supply.

ILKLEY

Ilkley is one of the most elegant towns in England situated at the foot of rugged Ilkley Moor with steep streets leading down to the banks of the Wharfe. This former Spa Town has retained the dignified air that would have once attracted the wealthiest people to this 'heather spa' in search of a cure during the Victorian and Edwardian era. It is a town of wide, tree-lined streets with old-fashioned shops especially along The Grove where you will find the world-famous Betty's Tea Rooms.

There have been people living in this area, particularly on the extensive moorland to the south of Ilkley, since the earliest times. Indeed, Ilkley Moor and Rombalds Moors boasts over 250 prehistoric 'cup and ring' carved rocks as well as stone circles, ancient enclosures, cairns and burial mounds. These mystical carvings can be found on large slabs of grit-stone in prominent positions overlooking the valley and on the highest ground. Perhaps the most enigmatic rock carving is that of the Swastika Stone, which is one of the oldest rock carvings in this country dating back to at least the Iron Age, if not the Bronze Age, and is similar to carvings found in Italy and Sweden. This symbol has been used in many ancient cultures throughout the world for thousands of years to represent the sun and good fortune, before the Nazis gave it a much more evil significance. The moor is also renowned for strange lights, unexplained shapes and UFO sightings!

In around AD80, the advancing Roman legions swept aside the native British tribes of Northern England, collectively known as the Brigantes, and established a fort known as Olicana on a small hillock overlooking the River Wharfe to protect the important river crossing, which forded the Wharfe near to the present 17th Century Old Bridge. The fort was originally protected by deep earthworks and wooden palisades, later replaced during the 4th Century by stone walls, a short section of which can still be seen behind the Manor House. A Roman civilian town (Vicus) grew up beside the fort, attracted by the soldiers and their regular pay packets. Little is known of its layout as much of the Vicus was built over during the 19th Century as Ilkley prospered and grew as a spa town, although discoveries indicate that The Grove follows the line of an important Roman road and that there was a Roman cemetery near the railway station. Little remains of this Roman fort and civilian town, although the Manor House Museum boasts a fine collection of Roman artefacts and also tells the story of the history of Ilkley through the centuries. The Manor House dates back to the 14th Century and stands on the site of the West Gate into the Roman fort, whilst All Saints Parish Church stands right in the middle of the fort. There has been a place of worship on this site since the 7th Century when a small stone church was built here using stones from the abandoned Roman fort. Inside the church are three intricately carved Saxon crosses that signify how important this religious site was in Saxon times. The church was largely rebuilt during the 1860s although some older stonework remains including the 15th Century tower and a medieval doorway, font and wonderful effigy of Sir Adam Middleton that dates from around 1320.

In the 17th Century a well was discovered on Ilkley Moor, according to folklore, by a shepherd who bathed his injured leg in the water and the pure water cleaned the wound and cured him! Encouraged by the rise in popularity of 'spa towns' during the mid 18th Century, especially nearby Harrogate, Squire Middleton created two open-air baths at White Wells in 1756; roofs and extensions were added in the mid 19th Century. The natural spring water that fed these baths was particularly cold and gave the bather such a shock that it was believed to have curative properties that could help cure everything from gout to melancholia! Ilkley soon developed from a small village into a fashionable Spa resort with large hotels, hydros and villas where wealthy businessmen and their families from the neighbouring wool towns and cities could come to recuperate, including Charles Darwin who visited White Wells in 1859. In addition to bathing in pure moorland spring water, the 'Ilkley Cure' included exercise, fresh air and a healthy diet - the perfect tonic to rid the system of the pollution from the industrial towns. White Wells Spa Cottage can be found on the slopes of Ilkley Moor overlooking the town; it still retains its cold water plunge pool. By the late 19th Century, the fashion for the 'cold water cure' began to wane and Ilkley became a popular holiday and commuter town. Ilkley is perhaps best known for the song "On Ilkley Moor baht 'at", the national anthem of Yorkshire - although make sure you wear your hat otherwise you might just catch your death of cold, especially after visiting White Wells!

Betty's Tea Rooms, Ilkley

LOG BOOK

Keep a record of your walk with this Log Book.

Stage One   *Date   Time started walk   Time finished walk*

Weather conditions

Lunch stop

Highlight of the day

Evening Accommodation

General comments

Stage Two   *Date   Time started walk   Time finished walk*

Weather conditions

Lunch stop

Highlight of the day

Evening Accommodation

General comments

Stage Three   *Date   Time started walk   Time finished walk*

Weather conditions

Lunch stop

Highlight of the day

Evening Accommodation

General comments

Top: Above Kettlewell
Middle: Lofthouse
Bottom: Thrope Edge
©Mark Reid 2006

Top: Yorke's Folly
Middle: Hag Dyke
Bottom: Gouthwaite Reservoir
©Mark Reid 2006

Top: Great Whernside
Middle: Thruscross Reservoir Dam
Bottom: Thornthwaite Packhorse Bridge
© Mark Reid 2006

Top: Angram Reservoir Dam
Middle: Scar House Reservoir
Bottom: Guisecliff
©*Mark Reid 2006*